I0422715

Education

The Education of Children
with Regard to Growth

*

essay

*

Traumear

Copyright © Traumear 2018

All rights reserved. No part of this publication may be
reproduced, stored in or introduced into a retrieval system, or
transmitted, in any form, or by any means (electronic, mechanical,
photocopying, recording or otherwise) without the prior written
permission of the publisher.

Paperback ISBN 978-0-244-69071-7

*

www.traumear.com

*

The education of children with regard to growth takes account of growth as necessary and unavoidable. We either cooperate with it creatively and thrive or we ignore and resist it and suffer dire consequences. A true teacher remains aware of this necessity in his pupils and he introduces them to their own ability to cooperate with it. This essay is therefore for those who are unhappy with what they are offering their pupils and who suspect that they are able to be true teachers.

*

Education

It seems of the essence that one has to be educated and that one has to educate oneself. Also it seems clear to some nowadays that education ought to go together somehow, at least in the mind if not in the classroom, with something called individual growth.

Now this business of growth can be pictured very nicely as an instinct in the child which is led by the adult. "Please, sir, I wish to walk. Which way shall I walk?" "This way, my dear." "Thank you, kind sir."

Individual human growth is not like that. It implies growth against something. A *countervailing* force has to be taken into consideration, otherwise the argument between learning by rote and learning by experience ends in stalemate. The drug and funnel method denies the individuality of the child. That much is clear. One may not be able to change it but at least one pays lip service and agrees that it is wrong. Especially if one is not a teacher.

The actual advocates of growth-education, on the other hand, sometimes overstate their case by talking as if, by removing all hindrances, they might get the educational mainstream to flow. One wonders how much magic or charisma has to be laid on before an individual can be seduced to function. That is strong language and I hope to quantify it later.

Generally what is meant by individuality embraces the concept of a singular and unique potentiality in each one of us which should be taken on trust. The metaphor of the seed is used, the acorn, except that no two individual human beings are as alike as two oak trees. So something else comes into it.

Let's for the time being call it the individual environment. Here is the teacher who intends to be all things to each man. But he wastes his time, because nobody needs all things for a comparison. We only need what suits us, what is appropriate. But what is that? How can anybody tell beforehand?

We ourselves know least of all. Can a man or a child educate himself if he doesn't know what circumstances would serve him best? Especially since what we like is not always what serves us well?

If education is to be more than a straitjacket or a balloon that will burst on impact, the pupil must have something to push against and this something has to be in a relation of sorts to the pupil. It's possible to learn in an academic environment. It's equally possible to learn within the context of an everyday existence.

But there must be an opposition. That does not mean to say that the opposition has to be provided. There will most certainly be opposition, then. Shall we put it that way? An imbecile teacher working for a purblind Education Authority is a sort of opposition to the pupil's growth instinct. So is the hill he has to climb on the way home and so are the artificial problems he has been asked to solve.

A god overcomes everything automatically. The individual human being needs something to overcome in order to be able to grow.

But why say that he needs it? He will get it in any case, won't he? Even the most indulgent and permissive teaching has to be overcome sooner or later. What exactly is at stake here?

*

School education is artificial, there is no getting around that, and we do well to keep it in mind when we discuss the teacher's role, and the aspect of that role which has to do with the presentation, to the child, of an element of *countervailance*.

Here we have it then. In life, it is the accidents that have to be overcome. We make plans, we realize them, except for the unforeseen, which we overcome. If we don't overcome it we get burdened or crushed by it. But the artificial school environment is an obverse of life – I mean by definition. It's the simple and usual outside and inside of art and life. The artificial situation lets us control our responses and practice our reactions to accidents, or rather to that which corresponds, in the pretend context, to what happens accidentally in life.

And here comes the crucial point. The countervailing mass is not the work, the exercises, the obligation to arrive at school and remain there, well behaved, nor is it the examinations and tests. These are not necessarily burdens at all, as we see in the cases where pupils tackle them as it were on the run. Nor do I mean to suggest that the countervailance, that against which the pupil best grows, is essentially an unpleasant experience.

But I don't want to reveal my top card yet.

The developing child grows towards personhood. A person stands 'in relation to', and is aware of that relation. A person knows he stands in relation to at least one other person. By myself I cannot be a person.

So the call of personhood is also the yearning to come out of myself, to be educated.[1] It's a fact that in an important sense a

---

[1] Elsewhere, in a much later essay, I have identified this 'coming out' as a repair strategy. To the extent that a child has been neglected and misguided rather than brought up, education becomes necessary. A well brought up child does not need to be educated. Similarly an immature adult, in order to be able to mature, must choose to come out of his self. The child is to come out of *himself*, the adult out of *his self*. The tragedy of modern life is that every system or institution creates the difficulties it promises to ease.

child knows everything. How delightful that one day he will be able to explain some of it to me!

But first the education towards personhood.

Towards what? The child is intrigued. He pricks up his ears. Towards what? He can't understand what we mean. He wants to be shown. It really lies outside his ken, this personhood. He can only make it out very dimly. Of course he isn't ready yet. But he experiences the thing nevertheless, almost as beyond him, but within him at the same time. Subjectively it's a desire, objectively a goal. The same thing, both desire and goal. The tension between the two – the tension and the suspension – there we have it finally, the element of *equipoise* and of *countervailance*. Goal and desire.

And the teacher himself is to supply it – in himself. That's my top card. The teacher has a unique skill. With him this skill stems from an organic need. He knows that he needs to teach, to be fulfilled, so he develops this need as a skill. He needs to teach until he actually does so, and once he does, he is free because he practices his skill. Freedom from need implies an activity, a work. It implies a degree of self-realization.

And the teacher realizes himself in a peculiar way while he teaches.He holds out this personhood which he knows and esteems and he holds it out in front of the child like a carrot. This is the real carrot of the educational process. And the stick? There's a stick too. It's what happens to the child while it doesn't rise to the occasion of this proffered personhood. While it doesn't rise to that occasion it experiences all those accidental experiences which have to be overcome, and which it may gladly overcome, so as once again to be in line with the teacher in terms of personhood, in a human relation towards maturity, both desiring personhood and enjoying the foretaste of it as a goal.

What does the pupil overcome? His failure to rise to the occasion and reality of the teacher's own proffered personhood. This proffered human relativity is the teacher's skill.

Of course the child needs something to aim at. Of course he needs something to spur him on.

Within the pupil-teacher relation we see the skill of the teacher, his fulfilling activity, and we see the maturing child, overcoming his unwillingness to be educated, which unwillingness exists in the first place because of the teacher's personal challenge.

It's enough for a teacher to be with a pupil for this educational process to be set up. Nothing explicitly needs to be done, except that the teacher should be who he is, the teacher. His work begins when he is with the child. Being a teacher is in itself skilful work.

There is the countervailance while the child says no to the teacher. The teacher sees this right away. In his awareness he takes note of how this element builds up. He isn't afraid of it, it doesn't make him anxious. Is the carpenter afraid of his chisel?

The teacher's skill responds victoriously to this need in the child to say no. He recognizes the child's healthy individuality. He welcomes the strength of the individual, he doesn't fear the rebellion of the 'brat'.

The rebellion of the brat is feared by the ignorant grownup. The teacher says an emphatic yes to the child's no and he calls the child courageous and plucky for saying no. But all the while he proffers his personhood which overflows in the teacher and flows out from him as an influence of life.

And here's another thing. The individual child has to say no to the teacher long enough until the particular quantity of countervailance has built up that will suit that particular child to overcome. Every child is different in how, and for how long, he says no to the teacher and meets challenge with challenge. The docile child is not engaged in the education process.

Please don't call it rebellion, this no-saying of the educable child. It has nothing to do with rebellion.

The child throws nothing back. It merely withholds itself from the teacher's peculiar influence. Suddenly the child is not 'he' but 'it'. The teacher senses it, this challenge of neutrality. Not only does he sense it but he gladly recognizes it – as the half of the education process.

The other half is equipoise.

One recognizes the teacher's kinship here with the creative art-worker, who has within himself that which in turns says no and then yes to the spirit.

*

When the pupil says yes to him, the teacher is not on that account elated or relieved. Again, he knows what goes on. The child has for the time being accepted and adopted the person-hood held out by the teacher. The child plays the game. Some-thing important goes on while the child plays along. It's enough that the pupil should not withhold himself for this something to go on. And really that's all we need to know. That's all the teacher needs to know, that the best possible thing goes on. He doesn't have to ask what it is. His procedure won't change, his approach won't be altered in accordance with what goes on. Nevertheless we may ask what it is that goes on and the answer will simply be that the child is learning. If that's too vague, since to some people learning has to do with memorizing data and drilling routines, then say that the child grows. He develops towards his adulthood. He grows up.

If at the same time he takes it in stride that 'the intensity of illumination varies in inverse proportion to the square of the distance from the source' then so be it.

We can distinguish between what and why the teacher teaches. Both of these are interesting enquiries, We need some conception of the why and of the what. Forget about the how for the moment.

Why does he teach? He would like to see the child grow up, to see his individuality unfold in as many ways as possible. It does the teacher good to see that come about and to know that he was instrumental in bringing it about.

What does he teach? Why, whatever seems most appropriate at the time. But will he not teach Geography? Or reading and writing? Or drawing and singing?

He won't teach those things because they are not to be taught. One cannot teach Geography or Physics or History. One *trains*, or is trained, in these.

The distinction between teaching and training is all-important here. Confound these two and you end up with several unnecessary and misleading problems on your hands. The mix-up of education with vocation results in a similar muddle, in untold complexity that leads nowhere.

*

So what does the teacher teach?

Of course a certain amount of training goes on.

"Heed me now!" That's training. Does it come first? Is that a priority? Not at all. The training follows. Also it accompanies the teaching. Why would the child heed the teacher if the pupil were not persuaded by the master? The pupil won't heed an ass, because an ass can't teach. Though the child might give himself the appearance of heeding the ass, so as not to get kicked.

So even training is no good unless it accompanies or succeeds teaching.

But the teacher could train the pupil in Geometry if he taught him first, or at the same time. The pupil would heed him in terms of Geometry, but for the sake of the teaching. Never for the sake of Geometry. How could he? What good is Geometry to him as an individual person? But he can sense the good of the personhood extended to him by the teacher. He soon develops an exceedingly fine sense for it. Once that sense is established, the teacher can teach in terms of anything he likes and 'whatever seems most appropriate'. I retain that phrase.

Because while the teacher offers the personhood at his command and as he chooses the terminology of Geometry, he is also organically present. We must be able to take that for granted, that the teacher is organically around, because he is not an 'ass' or a 'creep'[1]. These two don't know what organic presence is, but the teacher does, and he understands what it means.

It means first of all that he is aware of the fact that he sees and hears and feels. He is aware of himself as a looking, listening and touching 'being'. He is not conscious of this but aware; there's an important difference. The awareness includes itself in the transaction, consciousness can not.

The transaction? What is that now?

The teacher who sees makes it possible for the pupil to see. Right then and there the pupil becomes aware of the fact that the possibility exists for him to see.

---

[1] I offer these two terms wisely as definitions, not as insults. The ass brays and kicks and makes life difficult for himself and others; the creep tries his best to remain unaffected by his pupils. He is a functionary who prefers to remain -in a world of his own.

It's marvelous. Awareness is such a thing that it leaps right across. The child becomes aware without knowing what happens to him. He becomes automatically aware of the possibility to see. I know it's only the possibility. He doesn't automatically see. Seeing, like all the organic faculties, is voluntary and intentional. But good grief, how far is it from the awareness of the possibility to the actual grasping of the reality?

However, it may be more appropriate for the child to hear than to see, to feel than to hear.

The teacher develops a sense of fidelity. He is not a dog any more than he is an ass; a cynical cur lacks this sense of fidelity and he lays concrete where something might have been planted. The callous cynic is a dog with no conscience. But the teacher senses what is most appropriate at the time as he relates to the child. In terms of Geometry he may teach the child to see, to hear, to feel. These are the three most original faculties. We are talking about human beings, not elephants or dolphins.[1]

*

So now we know what the teacher teaches. He teaches sight, hearing, feeling. We will get back to that.

The teacher has nothing to do with the organic percentage of us. A teacher is not a trainer, not even a little bit of it. The trainer tricks the pony through the hoop. Then the carrot. Too easy? Why, smear pitch on the hoop and ignite it. No, no carrot until you hop through. But a stern look and a touch of the whip if you don't. And then what? After it leaps through the burning hoop, what shall the trainer do next? Look at my pony, not anyone else's, he shouts. But he knows that in order to attract the

---

[1] One makes these arrogant comparisons to animals. The relationship of a mahout with his Indian elephant is worth looking at. A good mahout does not try to force the obedience of his elephant. He appeals to the animal's humanity. Dolphins delight in being taught by someone with personality.

shekels he has to produce the goods. Results are what counts. Raise the hoop higher. Let the pony try it on three legs. Along a tightrope. – But then the poor thing has a nervous breakdown. It collapses from sheer imbecility – imposed imbecility. I think it was afraid of being trained in Mathematics next.

You can train the flesh, but first you have to kill the flesh; and then you have to lay down indisputable tracks. Those tracks are crucial. And once you have killed off the flesh, why it's obvious now that this dead flesh needs to be trained to be kept out of mischief and to give it a semblance of vitality. Those are the two tracks. Lay them over hill and dale, through mountain ranges and mountains, the rougher the better, because it gives us a semblance of vitality and then we can say we have merit, and we have deserved our carrot. Heaven help us that we should pick up a carrot by the way.

Or who needs all that vitality in any case? That's the other voice. Let the train drift, it will find its way. Buddhism cum mysticism plus leisurely charisma. – But that's training too. The carrot here is a negative carrot, a root made porous by root-rot.

No, there's no destiny on that train, neither in reverse nor forward gear.It's a sham train. The sooner we climb out of it the better. – "But it's travelling at such a devilish speed!" I hear you say. Fear not, it's a sham speed. Let your leap be real.

Why kill the flesh off in the first place? Why go to all this trouble for a sham vitality if the actual vitality already exists? These poor children! Look how active they can be prior to the school term. The poor parents don't know how to cope. All this real activity!

Right until late into the night. "Up to bed now, Johnny, for Christ's sake, I'm dead tired!" Johnny isn't tired. Johnny wants to conquer Abyssinia, he wants to annex the Northwest Territories. But it's ten o'clock in the evening and Mummy wants to watch News Night and Daddy wants to sag into the settee beside her and watch Top Gun or some such drivel, so naturally the flesh has to be killed. Johnny has got to be got under, under the thumb, under the covers, under the weather, anything just so long as there's no understanding.

The flesh of the parents was killed and they were trained, so now little Johnny has to be trained too. I'll tell you what, let's invent a disease and call it hyperactivity. It will mean that Johnny is too fast for his parents to catch. Perhaps we can blame the food he eats.

Above all let's not blame ourselves for not teaching him. Because if we taught him there would not only be no need to kill off the flesh but all that original vitality would automatically end up in harness. All you would see would be mind-and-body vitality. But that's too risky. Once we admit that, we condemn ourselves. And who wants to condemn himself? Rather continue fully condemned.

*

So your actual training in the case of an individual human being is fully automatic. Even better than the latest washing machine, because the dirty clothes have to be stuffed into it and the clean ones dragged out. And don't forget the Ariel.

> "All hail, great master! grave sir, hail ! I come
> To answer thy best pleasure; be't to fly,
> To swim, to dive into the fire, to ride
> On the curl'd clouds, to thy strong bidding task
> Ariel and all his quality."

"My brave spirit!" says Prospero. That's the true spirit of training while teaching goes on. It's a brave and plucky spirit, it hardly waits to be told and off to do it's master's bidding, with a spontaneity that is absolutely correct.

No fear here that Geometry will be mistaken for a thing in itself. Why, it simply lends us its terminology.

The Sciences, the Humanities, the Arts, the Fine Arts – what's the difference? It's education we're about. Physical Education, what's that now? Learn to play games? Beat the other team to glorify your school? Win trophies for the shelves behind the glass? No, of course not, who would suggest such a thing. It's all about – well – about fair play, and the competitive spirit and ... and fresh air, relaxation from the teaching of Geology and History.

But we've covered that. Physical Education, compared to what? Mental education?

Heaven preserve us!

If we teach in terms of the flesh, why not our own too?

This may take us too far afield. I hope not.

It's in terms of appearances, our popular teaching. Let's insist on being quite candid about that. Whether it's Mathematics or Geophysics or Drawing – if we, as teachers, get involved with these, then it's appearances we have to deal with. If we want to participate in the education process, as teachers, (I don't even mention pupils, though I might) then its the appearance of name and number, of rock and mineral, of line and shape that interests us. Your vocational mathematician is not a teacher. And these appearances are what we mean, collectively, by the flesh. We ourselves appear at times, in the flesh, if the regress called zombification hasn't fully undermined us yet.

So the consideration of Physical Education, of PE as it's called, has led us into a quick analysis of the difference between the use of a discipline such as Literature for education and its value as work for the purpose of earning money.

I think discipline is not a bad word for it. But others would do. The main point is, that the educator takes a stance in the vicinity of the 'discipline', while the Mathematician and the Chemist have made it their own. The teacher utilizes Botany and Zoology as contexts.

The teachers who have done me personally some good have done so while they utilized my immediate environment as context. I believe that teachers in days to come – teachers, not trainers – should distance themselves from Literature and Biology altogether and simply utilize the pupil's immediate and expanding environment. Our pupils know precious little about their own back yards but their heads are stuffed with academic abstraction. Of course they don't suspect it. Those who stand before them in the classroom perhaps suspect it a little, so they live in fear.

The context of a real education:

Children, I should like to teach you today, if you would agree to learn. What shall we use as our context? The tribes that live in reserves on our doorstep? How about the weather and the climate here these days. Or I'll tell you what, we'll talk about what you can remember. Imagine yourselves just born and in a trance before all this beauty outside your schoolroom window. Yes, do compare it to the beauty inside your schoolroom. Have you seen anything like it?

A pupil: My vision is blurred by all this light. I can make out an object or two.

A pupil: Everything moves when you look at it closely. I'd like to take hold of it. Or I'd like to move along with it.

A pupil: Dark and light. Dark and light. I want to dance and sing.

Teacher: Do it!

Pupil: I'll put it off for a while, until the urge gets stronger.

Teacher: Peacefully contemplate the order of yourselves in your surroundings. What can you remember now? Do you wish for anything at all?

A pupil: I recall waking up in my bed before daybreak. I heard birdsong, ever so clear and loud. I turned into a living crystal. I wish I could be such a living crystal again. Thank you. I experience it now.

Teacher: Your longing transformed your presence. You changed. You are now someone different. Would you like another name?

A pupil: My own will do, provided I don't rivet myself to it. My name is not my person but quite free from it. Lucy means nothing until I decide to step into those shoes.

*

There we had a glimpse of real education in progress. The context is discernible here and there, but mostly employed, used up. The teacher makes use of it sparingly. A little suffices. Her awareness remains sovereign. Her pupils imbibe that awareness. They rise to the opportunities of seeing, hearing and feeling. Look at it again. Is that not true? Something is actually being taught, and that is the being of those children, their being as sense and knowledge. Observe how they discover. Notice the gratitude.

*

I dare say we will have these sciences with us for some time yet, and people will continue to maintain that they 'teach the sciences and the arts', that they are 'Maths' teachers, and they will do it to "prepare the children for life, for the world, and for the job-market". These are the extinct sciences and the extinct arts, because they happen to be based on mere appearances and on the dead flesh. No need to quarrel with extinction. Far in the distant future I see the teachers who teach within a live context, the context of reality and truth. How nice if in the meantime one could see some evidence of this minor breakthrough, where the so-called disciplines, or subjects, are at least used contextually. I set myself this minor goal. Once we attain to that, the major goal of a live context can be approached right away.

Meanwhile, let's ask for teachers.

*

What to teach

The sensible being of a child is ever so teachable. My own sensible being is equally teachable. At this very moment I am being taught. I can only tell you it feels ever so right. The one who offers me his greater personhood also stimulates my senses.

But I want to take issue with this notion of a 'greater' personhood. It cannot be greater. What makes it effective for me is not any comparative size but that it is on offer. This is the fact that makes it so remarkable.

I learn. I place myself in the position of the learner. And the human being in person rises within me and offers itself to me in the flesh.

I accept. I am organic. If I did not accept I would not be organic and all my seeing and hearing would collapse into itself, would be blown away like chaff by the first wind of critical contention. My feeling would be futile.

So my organic being depends on the personhood I accept. I write from the point of view of the pupil now. I sense and I take pleasure in sensing. No pleasure so fine! No pleasure so comprehensive! My awareness plays over these senses. Thence this awareness? It flows into me automatically as I accept the personhood of the one human being. I mean the universal teacher. The one who teaches us all things.

He teaches us how to teach.

My context is language. In terms of language my senses improve, my being grows. I become more human. I sense the definite progress of my humanity.

Progress towards what?

Something takes shape under my hand. I am being taught, but at the same time I do work. Not only do I receive but I also give. Oh yes, I rely to some extent on what I wrote earlier, but that's no extinct science, it's live knowledge. No need to be chary with it; or generous, for that matter. It mixes itself in like air and it rises like sap. I call it my flesh and blood, this knowledge and here it gets worked into language – along with what I sense anew right now.

It's not enough for me to receive. I also want to give. No pupil is different in this. Prevent a pupil from giving and shortly thereafter he cannot receive. You may preach away at him until the cows come home but he will take nothing in. The educational transaction will not operate.

Suddenly I notice myself crouching into myself. I have to tend to myself now, I don't want to be influenced for the time being by my teacher and by his pressing need to teach. I want to get on without him, try my own hand, make a few mistakes, have a laugh or two. I don't know how far I'll get. I am still being supervised, but this I don't resent.

I sense the countervailance against which I strive. I understand what goes on. I am the willing pupil who insists on doing what he desires to do. My organic faculties have been stimulated and nourished, they have grown.

Now they want to be active. I let them disport themselves. My teacher watches. His awareness means everything to me. Nevertheless I make do with my own awareness now. That's how I make it my own. What I do cannot be done by anyone else, not now, not in the future. I do it so as to exercise my individuality towards my personhood.

My work includes you as a person, That's what it means to do work, to relate to another person, to several persons, as an exchange of life.

*

First and at the beginning I know that the teacher is present. Unless I know this he might as well not be present. I don't necessarily see, hear or feel his presence but I have knowledge of it nevertheless. But then I work from within a sphere of existence I call choice. The pupil who goes to school, by comparison, sees, hears and probably feels the presence of the teacher in the same room with him. The teacher knows how to take advantage of that knowledge, of that sense of his presence. Not that he has a high opinion of himself, this teacher; only a correct estimation. He is there as the teacher, not as the milkman or the banker or the parent.

So the teacher has a correct estimation of his office and of the difference this makes to the child, because the child will certainly know of the teacher's presence.

He will also soon enough know the presence of an ass. Or of a camel. A camel, or his cousin the chameleon, pretends not to be around, prefers to blend in with everything including the pupils, so that this valuable and fundamental tension due to the teacher's presence as teacher is lost or never comes about in the first place. The chameleon is one of the boys, one of the lads, he fools around on the same level because he can only conceive of the pupil-teacher relation as a two level thing, and he has had his fill of the authoritarian, bossy-boots approach, equally of the self-effacing, sacrificial baby-booties approach, and he is thoroughly tired of all that, so he 'comes down' to the level of the pupils and becomes in turn seducer, devil's advocate or Jack-the-lad.

So we need to identify clearly here the teacher's office, which has to do more with personal magnetism than with condescending despotism or the corporate build-up to which one is expected to defer. But it has nothing to do, all the same, with magnetism, or with the magic of charisma. These things are detrimental because they break down character and dissipate personhood. Let's say instead that the office of teacher is organically established and derived.

I compare it again to my own case. When I turn to the universal teacher I don't turn to an idea or an ideal, and I don't expect anything from an abstraction or from some ideological construct, nor do I look to an impersonal entity, a mere force or energy that somehow informs me, but I take a stand vis-à-vis the one who resides by choice within my own human being. Not within my popular being, where I want to get chummy and matey and secretly my own back, but within my human being, which is a highly specialized affair in the eyes of the people but to me it's the simplest thing again in the world.

And as soon as I take that stand, a profitable tension is set up between me and him. I realize that he has a will of his own and that my own will in turn diverges or coincides. (I steer clear on purpose of the mystical ideal here.) My will coincides or diverges, so we're back to the elements of countervailance and equipoise. There is attraction or direction, and work goes on in both cases. Teaching and learning are work. Not hard work, but pleasurable, enjoyable and satisfying. Training in the extinct sciences and arts, that's hard work. Teaching them, that's stultifying and shameful work. Why call it work? Call it servility and slavery, domineerance and subjection. Call it vile.

My will coincides or diverges, and when it diverges I am no less the good pupil. My teacher is more than his will. He is the truth and the light, the resurrection and the life, and he respects, he welcomes my diverging will. By going against his will I only practice what I previously learned from him.

In the instance of my own education too, therefore, I recognize the principle of counterpoise, and I notice what it has to do with the office of my teacher. The teacher in the classroom after all is informed by the teacher who is the spirit of truth. Their offices are alike.

The office of teacher as dynamic boils down, in the last analysis, to the teacher being present to the pupil. Look no further afield. Your credentials are your presence as teacher in the classroom with your pupils. Your credentials are not how quiet and orderly your pupils are, what sort of results they get to examination, neither are they your degree from the Training College nor your contract with the School Authorities via the Principal and the Board of Governors. These things are all appearances and of the flesh. An ass and a camel may acquire them. An ass throws tantrums and a camel has nervous breakdowns, right there in front of those pupils, because the tension is negative, it's not handled and employed. So what if you work in the company of a thousand asses and camels; you be a teacher!

These children in front of you, grouped silently or scattering noisily, will sooner or later ask you for your credentials. Then they will demand them. Especially the strong and healthy ones will demand them. They don't mind the company of a camel or an ass because they can cope with these. They are accustomed to the long dry spells and they know how to kick back, or to roll with the punches. What they cannot and will not abide, in their health and in their strong sanity, is the camel or the ass who gives itself airs of being a teacher. No, that is quite intolerable to them. It's a sickening sort of spectacle for them and they lose all respect, especially that essential self-respect they were born with. When that goes, they become restive. They stir up trouble. They even train themselves in the stirring up of trouble. And that is their way of demanding your credentials, as teacher.

*

A teacher ought to have some notion of the difference between live and extinct knowledge, otherwise he stumbles about in the dark, which he hates. The teacher has a hatred of wishy-washy concepts. He wants to be above all clear in what he does. So the very nature of knowledge is bound to intrigue him. After all it's his stock in trade.

He will tell you however that not everything he knows is taken straight out of books. When a teacher hears himself quoting from a textbook he recoils from himself and experiences a slight nausea. It's his conscience. He is being dishonest.

How is he being dishonest? As a teacher he has no business passing on second-hand goods. Never mind the quality of the textbook right now. The extinction resides in the origin of his message, and this origin lies outside of him.

Live knowledge originates within us. Extinct knowledge, if truth be told, doesn't originate at all but it lies outside of us. Enough said that it lies. It lies about all over the place and the textbooks are full of it and specialists in it abound.

But let's come to terms with it, if possible. It may prove difficult.

Is it extinct knowledge that four plus four is eight? Wait a bit. A child might well say: Four what? Four what plus four what makes eight what? What kind of a question is that? Easy with the abstractions now! The child who would rather hear of four balls than of four, of six sweets rather than of six, is not necessarily out of his mind. We may say that his mind has to be

20

trained so as to be able to cope with six independently from six sweets, but what if he were able quite readily to do that but for some reason he is reluctant to make a thing out of it? I suggest that this is the crux of the matter. Some things are so obvious that we don't even want to be told about them. Why not? Because it makes us look stupid? No. Because it actually makes us stupid.

It stupefies us, to have what is self-evident pointed out to us.

Before we are still relatively unspoiled by bad education, a great deal is self-evident to us and we thrive on it. More and more becomes self-evident. How delightful! Almost everything in our world is personable and courteous. I can recall how it was like that for me once, while I grew up during the early nineteen-forties in a country on the brink of extinction. Then commenced many years of mostly bad education. Today I know again what it means for my world to be self-evident. I had to unlearn massive amounts of bad education. It got so bad that I couldn't look at a cloud without becoming conscious of the processes of condensation and evaporation, without speculating on the integral and differential calculus of random vapour movement through a predictable matrix. Do you notice how that takes your head away?

Nowadays I can look at a cloud and feel joy, or it puts me in a sombre mood. Or I go back to fetch my umbrella. A lot of redemptive work has gone into that. I've had to forgive the poor benighted souls who filled me so full of trash until I didn't know who I was or whether I was coming or going.

All I mean to say is that reality is self-evident and one doesn't get any closer to it by trying to explain it in terms that are less real.

And yet, isn't that what ninety percent of our so-called institutional education amounts to: an attempt to explain and justify a self-evident reality in terms that are not self-evident but derived and contrived?

The child at his school desk is first made dull by this important-sounding voice telling him that four and four is eight. If he were told this as a joke he might be able to laugh it off but the voice is deadly serious. The voice may even be kindly-deadly serious, which is worse. Still worse, the voice may be spiritually-kindly-deadly-serious. Do you know what I'm getting at?

You, dear reader, are reading these words. You are reading them to yourself. You are probably sitting somewhere. You are sitting down. Sitting down is not like standing up. If you were standing up you would not be sitting down, but standing up. Who is talking back there! Jane, to the front of the class! I will have attention! Jeremy, what was I saying!

"You were saying that standing up is not like sitting down, Miss, but more like standing up."

"Good boy, Jeremy. But I did say: The one is the other, not 'more like' it. We must get this right if it takes us till doomsday, which, by the way, is only four weeks away and you will get essay questions, you may be sure of that. Once more, altogether now, especially for Jane, who seems to think that this is all so much nonsense: Sitting down is sitting down. Standing up is standing up. Loudly! All of you!"

The light goes out.
The light which once on early limbs
Fell indiscriminate,
Goes out.

Hatred and guilt
Breed morbid discontent
And a false standard
Squats on the senses.

*

22

A false standard for the senses – this is what develops if we make no effort, no good habit, of care for reality as self-evident. Reality reveals itself. It is willing to reveal itself. The nature of reality is such that we have to become obstructionist if we are not to be touched and moved by it. We have to develop negative and bad tastes and habits, eventually even to the point of addiction to these, if we are to prevent reality. We are always appealed to, we are forever approached from there.

This appeal, however, is to us as persons, which is to say as total individuals, all gathered together as thoroughly as possible at a certain time, and also as individual persons who extend themselves towards reality. Our part is to pay attention and to pay it fully, with as much of our being as possible.

And then, with reality reaching out towards us and we opening ourselves to it, we experience it as self-evident. "Of course," we say. "How else! I can see how it couldn't be otherwise. If it were otherwise it wouldn't be reality and my experience of it would not be real experience. And while I reach out to relate to this reality, I may actually call it personal experience, because that makes sense."

Now what happens is that someone comes along and tells me: "This is reality and I want to explain it to you so that you can understand it. This is because of that and that is because of the other. Reality is a code and I am going to help you crack that code. Then you'll be happy and powerful."

This makes me suspicious. First of all I find it tedious and I get bored. "Aha!" I say to myself. "This chap is trying to hoodwink me. Maybe he is fundamentally miserable and looking for popularity." When I look closely at what he calls reality, I discover to my astonishment that he means mere appearances. He means something that would at least be associated if he left it alone, but by touching it he dissociates the parts of it until nothing relates to nothing, except by way of his spurious explanation. "This is not really itself" he says importantly, "but it is that!" I reply: "Then what about that?" He says: "That is the other."

Ands so on, one presumes. 'The other' is something else again, but by that time one has become so stupefied that one asks no further. It's an explanation to the death. Dead ends are achieved and regarded as results and solutions and rewards. Meanwhile one has oneself become dead and is willing to recognize one's own.

Terrible business!

The specialists in this can't be made to see reason. We have to mollify them, to play tricks on them – anything to keep them out of our hair. I would even go so far as to appear to agree with them when they corner me because I really have no hope for them. The specialists in extinction are a breed all their own – self-bred, as it were – and my main ambition in relation to them is to protect myself against them. What really worries me is when I state my own case and they say that they agree with me whole-heartedly and that they're completely on my side. Well, I'm not on any side, and I don't want anybody on my side.

When we ask ourselves, or one another for that matter, what to teach, we have to have some kind of notion of reality, that goes without saying. I only say it because the opposite gets said all too often,

The simple answer of course is: Teach reality.

But the related question is: Whom to teach.

We teach reality and we teach pupils. We teach pupils to open themselves to reality, to reach for it, and we teach reality as the self-evident thing which by its very nature appeals to us.

Reality isn't hard. Our hearts are hard. We need to be taught.

24

We aren't bad. Our notions of reality are bad. We need to be taught reality.

Do we start with reality or ourselves? It really doesn't matter because you cannot discuss one without the other. But at certain times and in certain places, faced with one pupil rather than with another, it will occur to us to stress one or to emphasize the other, to put the accent on reality as the perceived thing or else to concentrate on the pupil as the perceiving human being or person. We mustn't attempt to do one in separation from the other, or to pretend that such a separation is possible. Where we, as teachers, lay the emphasis must depend on whom we are dealing with and on the context of the times.

*

Improvisation

One worthwhile approach to reality and to the perceiving person is improvisation. I am speaking now as a teacher, intent on practical achievement.

Improvisation, in this context, is a combination of illusion, imagination and calculation.

We understand that where someone has become unfortunately attached to a false reality, especially to a hypocritical one, there is no arguing with him, not on those grounds, because what he sees as real you see as false, and what you see as false he calls real. It stands to reason that without a common ground no consensus can be reached. If the nature of the mutual predicament had to do with the ripeness of tomatoes or the fiscal policy of the government one could hope to come to terms, but when the nature of reality itself is at stake, no such common terms are available, since everything we are and do is shot through and informed by how we view reality, whether we have ever really used that word or not.

Improvisation is the setting up, for the time being, of a true illusory reality, an antechamber to reality into which the light from reality shines.

The teacher is closer to reality and knows more about the sensible person than the pupil. And he also gets to know his pupils. So he draws their attention to something outside of themselves, to which they themselves have not contributed but to which they can relate.

Now everybody can relate to his own physical make-up and to his own mental constitution. We may not all know about coal mining or be familiar with double-decker buses but we all have mental capacities, however slight or aberrant, and we are all physically around somehow. (Ghosts don't count.)

A pupil, for one reason or another, may have very little genuine substance at his disposal. He may be overloaded with dead data due to bad Education. He may never have come up against a great deal of encouragement so that he is largely a puzzle to himself. Whatever the case, he will somewhere be capable of spontaneous growth. The teacher obviously assumes that the pupil will be better off under his influence or in his presence that if left to himself, and I mentioned earlier the office of the teacher as his exceptional presence. This assumption has to hold equal rank with the other one, namely that the pupil is capable somehow, who knows how and where or when, of a degree of genuine, spontaneous growth.

Does it make any sense to speak of such growth in terms of letters and numbers? or in terms of molecular models and quadratic equations? It could make sense, if the speaker were able to remain aware of the essentially mythic character of such concerns. How likely is that?

Where the teacher notices that a false sense of reality is established, he turns aside and continues to search for an as yet unspoiled faculty.

A pupil may show a natural bent to anger. Or he may incline to leisure. The teacher may notice a tendency to be readily swayed by suggestion. A desire to demonstrate, or to shine, may manifest itself.

These tendencies and inclinations however are such in the teacher's presence and under the influence of that presence, whether direct or indirect – whether the pupil yields or rejects. Outside the teacher-pupil relation these tendencies will not show up, or nowhere near as decisively. Others will be obvious then, however these mustn't concern the teacher.

Another way of approaching this tricky insight is to point out that the teacher, when looking for this so-called 'raw-material' sees nothing bad or negative, nothing that could be subjected to criticism by anyone or to flattery by anyone else. He looks for, and can therefore only discover actual, natural traits and definitely real characteristics. A child may be a confirmed thief in the eyes of the law and an inveterate liar in the eyes of his parents but the teacher sees none of this because he is completely engaged looking for something else, which will become plain to him sooner or later and which derives solely from the child's human being as manifested in the teacher's exceptional presence.

*

There is no reason why the teacher and the pupil should not immediately discuss what they discover during this introductory period of improvisation.

It's not as if some topic were introduced by the teacher or by the pupil and then it remained doubtful whether common terms could be supplied to make communication possible. Topics of conversation are like that. Or a teacher might try to predict beforehand what might work with that particular pupil, given his background, his ability and personality.

The improvisation I mean comes up with common terms first, within the dynamic pupil-teacher relation, and then a topic may suggest itself or, as I just said, the terms themselves might become food for discussion.

Remember that the teacher's prime concern is the proffering of his personhood. In his 'official' capacity as the present teacher he brings to play on the very nature of the pupil a desirable influence which, as we showed earlier, is accepted or rejected by the child. In either case the child is a pupil. In either case an awareness is transmitted.

If the teacher now decides to employ this method of improvisation, he will choose to depend on the pupil to reveal to him some aspects of his or her nature. It will not occur to him however to view these aspects as clinically removed from his own nature as that of the adult who is the teacher.

Improvisation involves teacher and pupils in their common human nature, and this human nature, which derives its initial impulse from the pupil (as the teacher intends), can itself become the model for perception.

But the teacher-pupil relation is specific. One enters into it for a specific purpose. This does not take away from the fact that teachers are born and that a child's nature lends itself readily to being taught. The child's nature may be overlaid by years of abstractionist sediment and the one who attempls to teach may be an ass; nevertheless a child's nature by definition and creation lends itself readily and offers itself immediately to a genuine teaching influence. Reality is what it is, appearances in line or out of line.

The pupil-teacher relation is specific and consequently the human nature that rises to such an occasion, being encouraged to rise to it by the teacher and initially stemming from, or taking its cue from, the child – is illusory. I refrain from saying 'only' illusory, because the illusion itself is specific. It makes sense that it should be illusory rather than factual. Whatever comes to the attention of pupils and teacher does so for the time being. Again I don't say 'merely' for the time being, since this time has its own particular content and end.

The end of it however lies outside of the specific encounter.

*

Illusion is an introduction to reality, like romance being an introduction to love. Any attempt to abide in the illusion ends in delusion. In the absence of an acceptance the invitation is withdrawn again.

The teacher comes to terms with the pupil on the instance of some genuine aspect of the pupil's original nature. The teacher looks for such an instance, he fully expects to be surprised by one. He never doubts for one moment that the pupil is capable of human being. This trust literally works wonders. A child may have gone on for years without a single manifestation of his human being and thanks to the trusting teacher something like a revolution takes place in him. One hears again and again from pupils who have experienced such a revolution in the presence of a trusting teacher. To them it may come as a revelation. They had forgotten what it was like to be spontaneous.

This introductory aspect then of what I mean by educational improvisation has to do with trust from the teacher, a manifestation of human being by the pupil and an illusion of common ground between the two.

Let's assume that the teacher continues in terms of this illusion. It is an illusion of reality, which is like a reflection of the light. In itself it makes sense only insofar as it leads somewhere, as a kindly light. The teacher of course is fully aware of this. If he were to walk away now, he would leave the child in the lurch. The unfinished business of the child's nature would swamp his imagination and leave him perplexed. The pupil would have on his hands a multitude of pictures and no method for dealing with these. An unnatural excitement would shortly be followed by a physical depression, long term apathy and a suspicion, by the child, that he has been fooled. He would be on his guard next time. A similar approach would understandably meet with a deal of resistance.

The teacher who stimulates the child and then leaves is a bad teacher.

Nevertheless some pictures are bound to be formed.

At the same time the trusting teacher may witness, in the child, the birth of imagination. Illusion is tended so that imagination may result. The child comes up with imagination as a human natural response, not to the illusion as such, as it has awakened in him, but to the illusion as tended and trusted and welcomed by the teacher.

To that end the teacher 'communes' with the pupil in terms of illusion, so that in good time the pupil's imagination may come to the fore. It happens in good time, and the teacher has no way of knowing that time. But he waits for it.

Imagination is the way we deal with our own insignificance in the light of reality. Reality encroaches upon us, we are insufficiently significant, then by way of imagination we make up the deficit. There is more to an imaginative person than to one who isn't. The concept of growth is all-important here, specifically of developmental growth. By way of imagination we develop. Body and mind both contribute, both are implicated, in the advent of imagination.

This is why the stimulated pupil would then be unable to cope with the real illusion in the absence of the teacher; he would be persuaded of this comparative insignificance as though it were really his own. Little does he realize that upon the onset of reality we are all at least momentarily insignificant. How can we expect him to do other than to put this down to his individual nature?

Bad education is worse than none because it destroys trust even as it originates in a lack of trust. A little education may be dangerous but any amount of bad education is downright destructive.

The teacher is aware of the need to wait for the first signs of imagination. While the pupil in his care may be bound by a history of delusion and deception, the teacher knows that trust is of the essence. In the case where he has decided to improvise, which we study at the moment, he places his hope especially in that part of the child's nature which we might call a willingness to play or a sense of play. Improvisation is an art and has to do with the teacher's art, more so than with the educator's science. Once we have dealt with improvisation sufficiently, we may take a look at another tack a teacher may take, where he emphasizes his dependence on the pupil's inquisitiveness and his sense of achievement.

Again, there is no need to separate the sense of play from the sense of achievement in practice. In any case, it can't be done. The distinction between the two has to do more with our study and understanding, because we want to know what we do while we do it..

The sense of play and the desire to question are linked in us like being and doing. We know that being is itself a fundamental kind of doing and that doing certainly implies being; nonetheless we distinguish between the two so that we may relate and communicate in the light of day. In that same light of day we also have two eyes, two hands and two feet.

The fact that 'illusion' is equated in common usage with delusion, with deception and trickery shall not deter us in this case. In the vernacular you can delude someone but you cannot *illude* him. Common usage has sometimes to be set aside. The teacher thinks highly of the sense of play of which the child may be capable and so he makes allowance for it. He does so quite seriously because he cares for his pupil.

Those who levy the charge of insincerity and falsehood at illusion do the same at dramatic acting. It should be possible henceforth to ignore them, but we see how their generation (the adulterous generation) has infected even our language. If a child pretends, and if he pretends to be a postman, or a bird, should we chide him and set him 'a proper task'? Surely such correction is fitting only where sheer fantasy is removed from reality and made to depend on itself in isolation, as in the case of the media.

If the teacher comes up with no affection for his pupil, he has lost the game in any case. We have to do here only with the teacher who improvises for the sake of the child, not in order to indulge a fancy.

*

How does illusion give birth to imagination?

The mind needs to concentrate. A plurality of pictures is experienced as digressive. Our nature demands order.

The human nature which manifests itself as illusion, given a degree of attention and care, becomes imaginative because otherwise it would digress and regress.

The teacher assumes that the child would rather grow than not grow. This assumption is both wise and very much to the point at this stage.

The teacher knows for a fact that human nature must be educated and that it wants to be taught. Notice the difference between teaching and education.[1]

Improvisation concentrates on teaching, on the fact that human nature wants to be taught rather than remain in ignorance. Knowledge is what allows human nature to grow, hence the pupil desires knowledge. He may manifest this desire in the way he rejects a false education. But the progress from illusion to imagination lies in the nature of human being – as observed during the pupil-teacher relation by the teacher. Outside of that relation, illusion and imagination can coincide or replace each other or even be absent. However during this improvised relation, the very illusion which supplied itself as common ground for further teaching becomes imagination once it has been sufficiently tended and thoroughly sustained. On the child's part we may speak of a playful drive and on the teacher's part we have a careful concern.

How should illusion be handled? Not at all. It tends to confuse us when we try to handle it. Compare illusion to a reflection in water. What happens to it when we attempt to grasp it?

Peace is important. Both pupil and teacher may learn to value what they do have in common here. Both may appreciate the crucial importance of not rushing, of not falling behind. Impatience and laziness are equally destructive. Never would the teacher be critical of impatience or laziness in the child however, since he knows full well how the relation is communal, not teamwork. He may guard against impatience and laziness in

---

[1] It would amount to the same if we said: The child must be withdrawn from whatever obstructs his human nature and taught to abide by his nature.

himself but he could never detect it in the pupil, as he could if he were involved, with the child, in a common task. This is no task, but more like an experience, where the obligation rests upon the teacher, along with the responsibility for success and failure as these in turns arise.

Peace and patience are maintained by the teacher:

Teacher: You sit there and your eyes are open, but I wonder, are you awake?

Pupil: I feel myself drawn – towards something.

Teacher: Describe it, maybe, as the longing for some kind of resolution. You get older. But you want to get wiser too. Small wonder that you …

Pupil: Don't make me uncomfortable. In my present state nothing seems certain, but nothing seems uncertain either. I express myself and that seems right.

Teacher: Fanciful notions occur to me, left and right, but I reject them. I feel perfectly at ease in your company.

Pupil: We have an hour together. During that hour I want to take advantage of your being here. I can sense that you know what goes on when we talk. You don't make me feel small, or insignificant. I can relax. I can be who I am without anxiety over who I ought to be, in your eyes or in anyone else's. This is important to me. You don't even need to talk. I seem to thrive on the way you listen. In any case, we are not on opposite sides. Neither are you on my side, nor am I on yours. These are valuable insights I am having. I find it very useful to be able to state what I mean. Are you tolerant?

Teacher: Tolerance has perhaps only very little to do with it. My ambition as a teacher is to establish a realm of secure advancement for those who agree to be my pupils. I would rather be active as a teacher than, say, as a mountain climber, and I take much pleasure in activity. If you were to refuse to be my pupil, someone else would step into your shoes. So I have nothing to fear from you but a great deal to gain. How about that?

Pupil: That lifts a burden from me. And it eases my conscience. Knowing that teaching fulfils you, I may learn in freedom.

Teacher: Have you learned anything so far?

Pupil: I have learned to keep still in the presence of my teacher, inwardly still, while matters that have proved difficult until now imperceptibly arrange themselves – in an order I could not have predicted. This inward stillness seems in itself to be productive. Would you suggest that I might do well to persevere in this inward stillness?

Teacher: The fact that you ask my advice cheers me no end. It means that you have gained a perceptible degree of confidence. What I may do is praise your elegant articulation of that question. Beyond that, your stillness is mine, mine is yours. We take no pride in remaining still but we announce the peace we discover. It guides us forward. Where it vanishes we right away undertake to regain it.

Pupil: I think you want me to continue to look beyond it. Am I right?

*

An illusion, or rather illusion itself, nothing definite, underlies this conversation. The pupil knows he depends to come extent on the teacher but he realizes he is all the more free for that. No topic as such is being discussed but as it happens there is mutual reference to 'how we are', to 'how things are going'. The teacher takes care not to break through the illusive shell; we notice his tact, his respect for the pupil's humanity. We have evidence that this shell is not a confinement imposed by the teacher but a natural production by the pupil, who expresses how he feels himself drawn towards something and then insists on his own way of putting it when the teacher suggests a description, an explanation of this. The pupil rejects the explanation of what he feels is self-evident. It makes him 'uncomfortable' to have the self-evident reality of the illusion explained. The teacher in turn understands this right away and deals with his own discomfort, so that he can honestly say that he feels at ease.

The teacher does not want the pupil to feel insignificant but he understands what imagination is and that it cannot arise in the pupil during a state of self-satisfaction. Complacency rules imagination out, but anxiety prevents it. So the teacher welcomes the pupil's expression of 'seeming' insignificance, his recognition of the value of 'stillness' and especially the fact that the pupil questions the nature of this stillness. Insignificant in itself, it leads on.

One can sense the following:

Teacher: I agree. The stillness you mean is like a pause in the conversation which one should not try to fill but from which one may expect the next item. Never be afraid to wait if you have nothing to say. And wait for the still peacefulness in yourself to reveal itself as sense. How much better to remain quiet together than to compete in terms of nervous nonsense! (a long pause)

Pupil: I have one thing in mind but another thing I feel. To which should I give precedence, to body or thought? I want to be able to make sense. It's like an ache in me.

Teacher: That makes sense. You refuse to be one-sided. You have notions in your head and pressures in your heart. The two refuse to fit. What's the typical reaction?

Pupil: From past experience? Either to give vent to the pressure against my better judgment and end up feeling guilt – or else to spin out some excitable notion divorced from the heart only to end up ashamed of myself. Guilt and shame have alternately been my lot in the past. There must be another way! I can't believe passively that nothing better is possible.

Teacher: You have what it takes to believe actively.

Pupil: How do you know that? How can you say that?

Teacher: Do you mean what right have I to pronounce on your capabilities? Only the right of the teacher, who limits himself in such things to the concrete human substance. We are all human, rather than not human; if not in reality then at least potentially, and on that score we have certain things in common. One of these things is the ability to believe actively. How you do that, whether or not you do it, when and under what circumstances – this has to do with your individuality, in which you are unique, not like anyone else. On your individuality I make no pronouncement whatsoever. That's your own business. I have by far enough to do in attending to my own.

Pupil: I believe actively that nowhere on earth have I so much to gain as right here right now. On this very spot at this moment I am what I am to the full. And do you know what? On account of your presence here I feel obliged to continue to be what I am to the full. This strikes me as rather odd. At least it sounds odd when I hear myself say it. How can I possibly …

Teacher: You get energy. Automatically you come up with strength. Never question the reason for that. It muddies the spring. Only persevere in the interest of yourself as an integral being.

Pupil: Then I have to distance myself from you. We are not any more on the same common ground.

Teacher: Which is only as it should be. Now assert yourself as flexibly as you know how. Tell me about yourself. When will you rid yourself of this servile tendency and trust that you can make up your own mind? When will you penetrate the cocoon of your emotion and annex the territory that is yours?

Pupil: That's a tall order. I recognize your appeal to my integrity, your demand on my character. I see no reason why I shouldn't respond to you exactly as I see fit. If you fail me now I will never forgive you. (Under ordinary circumstances I would have said that under my breath.) If I really begin to do what you suggest I do I am bound to hurt feelings, to make a fool of myself. It cuts both ways. I stand exposed now, and I speak for the first time, instead of just talking. Do you bear with me? No one has ever borne with me so far. Whenever I have made the slightest attempt to speak out in the past, I have right away been hushed. I didn't dare persist. Now I persist. You can count on me now to tell you exactly what I think and how I feel. If I can't do that with you for a while, using our association as a practice ground, I have no hope.

Teacher: You yourself are the one who interests me. Unless you speak out, honestly and sincerely, I cannot function now as a teacher. Hear what I say. Take from it what you can use. Soon we will undertake a project. First I want to be persuaded of your personal authority. Your authority accumulates as you learn to function spontaneously. I have faith in my own powers only because I've managed to sustain a multitude of blows to my self-esteem. Such conceit as a teacher comes up with – before he rejects it, frequently under duress – would be difficult to countenance by a non-teacher. Don't imagine that I sit here with all my problems solved. I only have a few more keys to solutions than you do. But then I also have more problems, so it evens out.

Pupil: I imagine that the cellar is full of rats and that the attic is full of spiders. Snakes and scorpions populate the other floors. Nevertheless this is my house and I intend that eventually it should be my home. I imagine now that I have what it takes to accumulate what is mine. If you stand by me for a while I promise not to lose heart.

Teacher: You can count on me, even as I count on the one who teaches me.

*

Imagination comes to our rescue at the appropriate moment. The teacher plans for it. The teacher hopes to succeed in terms of imagination. Where he improvises one might say he makes room for imagination.

One can tell in the previous exchange how imagination allows the pupil to draw on his own resources. As soon as he shows a willingness to do that, the teacher agrees to leave behind the previous illusory ground. He relies on his own resources too now. Shadow and light alternate. He actually abuses the pupil on one occasion when he tells him to catch himself on, to pull up his socks, and this has the obvious salutary effect. One should however take heed of the fact that what I call abuse here was not calculated.

Or was it?

Is the teacher not aware how each one of us first rejects imagination? Does he not realize that at once even an element of shock is required if our natural tendency to adhere to the past, to the illusory ground in this case, is to be overcome by our equally natural desire to grow, in this case to grow into express vitality?

The pupil seems to have acquired a fear of his vitality. Reluctant to say what he means, he cowers instead. One notices a tremor in his speech faculty. Where he senses the teacher's combined resources he rises to the occasion however. The teacher, as he senses, uses imagination himself, so it must be alright. A relationship of reliance is established, first by the pupil again, who nearly demands the teacher's support, as he ought to be able to do, then by the teacher in a subsidiary role, as he admits to what extent at this stage too his ability to function satisfactorily would be impaired by the pupil's unwillingness.

This relation of mutual reliance is then explored and exploited. As soon as the teacher is persuaded that the pupil operates from his own individuality, showing a modicum of authority, he begins to <u>calculate</u> in terms of a project.

Now for the first time can we say that there exists an external educational context. In order for it to be educational, this project has to arise imaginatively out of the teacher-pupil relationship. The fact that the teacher comes up with it is important. Had he suggested it earlier the pupil would not have been able to cope. Now the pupil trusts him. Also the pupil feels now that he can make use of the teacher, most importantly that he can say certain things to the teacher that have to do with his inner development.

Not until now does the pupil really begin to learn. With the advent of imagination an inner receptive organ has become established.

Learning has to do with knowledge, and knowledge in turn is our human body. Until we have a human body of knowledge we are carnal-accidental creatures in terms of mechanical control. This mechanical-material control is either imposed by ourselves or by others, it makes no difference. What matters is that we cannot behave in awareness and wisely. It's not that we won't, but that we cannot.

The majority of the children in the classrooms of our schools cannot learn. They have never been endowed with the organ for learning. This organ is a gift from the teacher to the pupil. In order to even exist organically, a child has to be brought face to face with his individuality by the teacher who knows. Those who don't know can't teach, that's obvious. Knowledge presupposes an organic awareness, however that organic awareness equally presupposes knowledge. Which goes to show that a teacher is necessary.

Except for the knowledge of the teacher, organic awareness is not possible in the pupil. The blind continue to lead the blind.

So it's all up to the teacher to know and to be organically aware. By way of improvisation he creates an environment within which the child may become a pupil. A gradual transformation has to take place if the child is to become active as a pupil. This takes time. The teacher takes stock of progress towards the child's pupil-awareness. How thoroughly does the child rise to the occasion of the teacher's, presence? Is there a tendency in the child to wait until he is told what to do? Perhaps he has become thoroughly accustomed to be told to sit down, walk in line, keep quiet, respond by rote and react predictably, so that in the presence of a teacher this same child is at first thoroughly confused. But the teacher persists. He has only one thing to offer, and that is knowledge. Unless he imparts knowledge he achieves nothing. But the imparting of knowledge has nothing to do with data from the external world. Such data illustrate knowledge once it has been acquired.

*

The teacher knows he has knowledge. His is a body of knowledge. That this knowledge should be imparted to his pupil is his foremost concern. He himself gains greater knowledge by imparting it.

Imagination could be called the aspect, or portion, of knowledge that makes it communicable. Once both teacher and pupil are able to communicate imaginatively and if improvisation is the teacher's chosen method – the next step is something that may be called <u>calculation</u>.

Imagine the teacher whose house is in order. His pupils go in and come out as they please, assured of respect, secure in their roles as learning individual human beings.

Should we not say that the pupil plays a role? It depends on what we mean by that. Certainly the child is not always a pupil, only while in the presence of the teacher. And the teacher is a teacher only while with the pupil. The pupil seeks knowledge, the teacher desires to impart it. They don't meet on the street and become teacher and pupil on their way to the post office. No reason why Jack and Mrs. Jones should avoid companionship or even friendship outside the classroom and off the school grounds. But once the teaching and learning start, such friendship and companionship are overridden and superseded by the teacher-pupil relationship, where each comes to play a particular and specific role.

Both should know about this. Both will eventually cultivate the specific nature of that relationship. Correct behaviour, fitting to the task, facilitates success.

Correct behaviour – that sounds most unusual. It reminds of morals and manners. Except that the task is not a social task. The task is an inward renewal and an outward testimony. The pupil has accustomed himself to the presence of the teacher and knows how to rise to the occasion of the relationship as soon as a session of teaching and learning starts. He wastes no time pretending to be other than a pupil while the teacher immediately falls in with the request of the pupil to be taught. This relationship, once entered, must be sustained and managed. The pupil sustains it, the teacher manages it.

How does the pupil sustain it? Through taking pleasure in it.

Oh rank infidelity! Is he not to be coerced then? Is he not to be loaded with chores, stretched on the rack between guilt and merit, between shame and the glittering prize?

The pupil automatically takes pleasure in his role as a learner. That's why we say that he plays that role. Otherwise the relation won't work. And the relation has to work, not the pupil or the teacher.

This sounds even more absurd. What, the teacher not work! The pupil not work! That goes against the very ethic of our western mentality. Whether it fits in with any eastern mentality I am not prepared to say.

The pupil-teacher relationship works – that is to say, knowledge is imparted, or transferred, if you like – while the pupil sustains it and while the teacher manages it.

No need for the teacher to strain his nerves and then to make the pupil suffer for it. No need for the pupil to slave away at his drudgery and then to despise the teacher for it.

The pupil actually takes pleasure in the relationship as the attentive learner. He mingles his faculties with those of the teacher. Since he accepts the lead of the teacher, and since this gives him more pleasure than if he rejected that lead, he is continually stimulated in his senses and repeatedly urged by the lead, he is continually stimulated in his senses and repeatedly urged by the impulse to make sense. The teacher's greater knowledge is the cause of that stimulation and it creates those impulses. That is the sort of thing knowledge is, and that is how it effects us.

*

Meanwhile the teacher manages the relationship. Certainly he understands that if the relationship is to work, he himself must believe that it will work. He does nothing half-heartedly. But he knows the difference between himself as Mr. Jones and the role he plays as teacher. While he teaches he does not stop being Mr. Jones. So he views his role as teacher from the point of view of someone who dispenses knowledge, while he never forgets that this knowledge must be imparted if he himself is to increase his own. We have mentioned this before, that the teacher imparts knowledge in order to increase his own. His body of knowledge is his body.

The teacher too plays a role. He plays insofar as he leaves to the expediency of the moment how best to comport himself. He tends to the pupil-teacher relationship. In addition to making his personhood available he serves that relationship in whatever way appears most advantageous at any given moment. Never does he impose his own will or insist on his own direction unless his conscious awareness first informs him clearly of such a direction. And his conscious awareness is of the pupil-teacher relationship. How well we can read a story to a child while we include that child in our experience of the moment! But once forsake the child and our words fall on deaf ears. The child's curiosity flags or becomes morbid. In both cases something ir-relevant goes on and regression, not progress, is the conse-quence.

In a similar way does the teacher arouse, by renewed effort, the teaching-environment. He has passed from illusion to imagination. He has made it his method to improvise rather than to experiment. Now it occurs to him to draw to his aid such symbols as allow his imagination naturally to express itself.

And then he calculates the relevance of those symbols.

Imagination moves with the times, we say. An absent-minded, inattentive adult has nothing to teach. Ordinarily magination, in order to function, takes hold of external sense data and orders them to suit itself. We may pretend otherwise but that doesn't change the facts. All facts are symbolic. They arise out of a confrontation between human imagination and the present light of day. Facts are due to an active imagination. We ourselves act imaginatively and are presented with symbolic fact. External sense data do not make an impression on us; they arouse our imagination which in turn gives us our environment. Our environment is not made up of sense data; it occurs to us as symbolic reality, which is calculable. What we calculate is the relevance, to ourselves and to those who depend on us for one reason are another, of those symbolic facts, those real symbols, and then, once we have managed to establish that relevance, we behave and conduct ourselves in accordance with what we call our environment. My environment can never be yours. There is no reason why it should be. What is ours is the result of any exchange. Communication allows us to live in the same world. In the absence of communication there is only a plurality of environments.

The teacher therefore plays his role astutely. He refrains from assumptions as to the pupil's environment. Instead he calculates the relevance of his own creative imagination.

It should be stressed here that he does not judge such a relevance. He passes no judgment on anything. The difference between judgment and calculation here is crucial. Judgment would have to be according to some standard, or final. We know that no standard can exist where creativity is concerned, and naturally the process of imagination is ongoing and not final.

So it all has to do with expediency, with what works best. The relationship works, the teacher selects. While the teacher remains within and below the relationship so to speak – and at its service – he cannot make a wrong selection and he knows it. He does not select according to external criteria but as the managing teacher. He uses his head organically, not like a moralist. Whatever he brings to the fore as worthy of attention is sure to please the pupil because, after all, the pupil has helped to create it by way of his own imagination.

*

The teacher calculates how best to imagine the world that is finally to surround him. By this world I mean a setting for the pupil-teacher relationship. The imagination especially of the pupil, but in combination with that of the teacher, reaches out to become real in the light of day. It reaches out in so many ways that the ingenuity of the teacher is kept busy because, as anyone well knows who has ever been in a position where children have depended on him, the way a child's temperament disports itself once it senses an atmosphere of liberty can strike terror in the unprepared soul.

The teacher of course has intended all along that the child should arrive at this point where he senses real liberty, so that certain rudimentary faculties should be exercised and new ones established. It would be safe to say therefore that the teacher's soul is prepared. He has striven for the possibility of such an outburst of emotion, he has persevered in the direction of the likelihood of such desires, he has urged the probability of mood, manner and thought. Finally the pupil cannot help himself but he lives. His being bursts the confines of his existence and expands into the space made available by the teacher. The teacher is bound to be ready.

Nevertheless even the teacher is surprised. The bad teacher is frightened and 'puts a stop to such nonsense'. The disciplinarian thanks his lucky star that he has measures at his disposal for 'nipping such an outrage in the bud. The authoritarian 'comes down hard' on what he cannot fathom since he was not involved in its inception.

But even the teacher is surprised, though rarely is it other than a glad surprise.

Finally then there exists a setting for the pupil teacher relationship. The pupil sustains the relationship while the teacher manages it. Again it's up to the teacher to await the spontaneity of the child. There may be long silences, lengthy periods of quiet while apparently nothing gets done, but these are times of productive calculation. Soon enough the child signals his readiness to proceed to some outward area of study. There is something like a leap of faith, when the child, who has until now remained wisely inward, takes an interest in outward things, not any more in playful mood but as serious study.

This passage from inward to outward experience is critical. When the child sees and hears now, he sees and hears what is and not what he senses. He feels what is and not what he senses. Sensation is indiscriminate and general. Seeing and hearing, feeling and touching, are specific and particular.

The point is not easy to grasp. Think of the difference between seeing what you generally and indiscriminately sense and seeing what there is. Once you see what there is you do not stop sensing but your eye, your organ of sight, has turned outward.

Inwardly you sense, outwardly you see, hear, feel etc. Don't confuse this with being either turned in or turned out. Extinction is a preoccupation with externals at the expense of the inward, so that there is neither sense nor sight. Education, by comparison, leads us out from a preoccupation with what we sense to the point where this is involved in what we outwardly see and hear.

Does the uneducated individual not hear or see, then? Not really. He hears or sees what he senses, and what he senses is not personal but general, not specific but commonplace.

Unless, of course, the uneducated individual is extinct, in which case he neither sees nor senses but there is only reaction to data and apathy before the elements.

How many of our schools cater to extinction!

If a child's so-called education has really been a path to extinction, can anything be done for him?

Not at all while the child has espoused willingly the system that holds him there.

But if that child rejects the extinct system and rebels, there is hope for him.

He responds to hope that comes to him by way of his inner life. His inner life has not quite been eradicated. Inwardly he is willing to lean in the direction of education, but outwardly he senses only the risks of an extinct education. Inwardly he is still open to the teacher-pupil relationship as we have described it. He is still willing to learn because he has not yet been completely undone to the point where he has begun to make common cause with those who have undone him.

*

Experimentation

The pupil is weary and wary. He crouches in himself, suspicious of anyone who tries to come close to him. He insulates himself in a mood of indifference or he acts out an image, something he hopes will confuse the opposition. The pupil who feels he himself is being opposed – given he has character – practices subterfuge. In this the pupil is not different from anyone else who has character and is being opposed. I should add that the opposition has been misjudged to be insuperable.

Let's not speak of the pupil but of the child. Every child wants to grow whether he knows it or not. There is mental, physical and spiritual growth. In all of these the child wants to grow. This growing is an organic necessity. We know all about it when it comes to plants and animals. They are different enough from us, so our sovereignty is not threatened. When it comes to our children, problems arise. By growing they seem to challenge our authority, our seniority, our superiority. There is the psychic complication of our wanting to get our own back, because at that age we weren't allowed to grow. Sounds fantastic? Think about it.

Not that thinking about things necessarily gets us anywhere. Wrongly we call it thinking when we justify ourselves, when we disguise our errors, when we insist on our rights.

The unfortunate child is opposed in his very own self. "You exist," we say to him. "Therefore we have to keep you in your place. Just like we are being kept in our place. And just like we were kept in our place when we were your age." And then comes the punch-line: "In order to keep you in your place we will send you to school."

The fortunate child is not sent to school for that reason. The fortunate child is promised an education and he gets it. His teachers trust him just as his parents trust him, not because he is trustworthy but because the atmosphere of trust is educational.

Who knows how to do that anyway, to trust actively, not to judge first and then trust if it's safe to do so? Every teacher knows how to do that. No bad teacher does. Bad teachers harbour a secret fear and a secret contempt in the face of their charges and they have to work hard to keep that secret well hidden, especially from themselves.

A pupil annoys those around him because, in his eyes, they succumb to the system. Maybe by now he makes snap judgments and all opposition scares him. He hasn't acquired the skill to operate against odds because any confidence he might have had has been knocked out of him by the insuperable odds of an impersonal, repressive system. From that point onwards, if something so much as goes against his grain, he right away hits back. He is becoming less educable in the light of what was discussed earlier as the principle of counterpoise.

The question is: How can one win back his confidence? His outside, extinct cockiness is a mask of confidence. For him it's better than nothing but for us, especially for the teacher, it's evidence of what is missing, namely real confidence.

Why not believe the mask for a while? I mean genuinely believe it. That does not mean that the teacher is taken in by it. On the contrary, those who repress that cockiness, and punish it, or sneer at it, are taken in by it because they treat it as though it were not a mask but something real, something genuine, when in fact it's only a symptom of fear. No doubt it disrupts. Masks can cause havoc among those who don't see them as masks. Even at a play where masks are used, an intelligent audience is not taken in by them. Our capacity for aesthetic appreciation proscribes the ignorant media response, which is no response at all but a dissipation of individuality.

To believe the mask means to take it for what it is, a mask, which implies ones awareness of the energy behind it, which, in the case of our pupil, is the negative energy of fear. As soon as the teacher realizes that the child is afraid, his heart goes out to him or her. He then deals with the fear and leaves the mask to its own devices. He helps the child deal with the fear and so wins back his confidence.

I would go so far as to say that only by believing the mask can the teacher take it for what it really is, for nothing more and nothing less. If he pretends it isn't there, he deprives the child of a needful protection and the child will feel tricked, even betrayed. Indeed it involves a kind of treachery, this so-called psychological insight which peeps behind the scenes and criticizes the performance. All it takes is the mere suggestion of "you can't fool me" and the child builds automatic resentment – unless the child is so gifted that he forgives the grownups everything out of hand; and there are such children, but then their confidence is not eroded in the first place.

If the grownup doesn't want to be fooled or duped, he has to believe the mask, whether that mask is produced consciously or unconsciously, in full awareness or as accident, as happenstance.

And still on the topic of masks, here too it helps if we can distinguish between being and doing. The rowdy who upsets the classrooms with his antics of provocation and disobedience is 'doing' a mask, while the withdrawn 'wimp' with the speech defect is 'being' a mask. Masks are half security-cover and half attention-seeking devices. But it has to be the right sort of attention. The introverted pupil, rather than throwing the enemy off his track, has learned how to keep out of harm's way, somewhere inside himself, and the speech-defect let's us know that the child is not 'intact', just as his rowdy brother's bad habit of destroying things testifies to a concealed pain. The mask of being would tell us: 'I'm alright, just leave me alone', but cannot help telling us at the same time: 'The right sort of attention would help me come out of my shell.' The mask of doing tells us: 'You can't injure me, I've got what it takes to defend myself', but at the same time it says: 'I hurt, I am miserable, at this very moment'.

The worst teacher is the one who manages to enlist the subterfuge faculties of the problem child in his own, the teacher's, interest.

Keep in mind what the bad teacher's interests are. They are order and discipline, well-mannered behaviour and diligence, obedience and initiative. In other words: Leave me in peace to get on conveniently with what I'm paid to do.

51

But these are all upstanding respectable qualities! Why, some of them are virtues!

The point is that they have nothing to do with teaching and learning, nor with education. From the teacher's point of view, these can be observed to come about while he teaches and while the pupil learns. But the bad teacher aims for them. He makes them his priorities. "First," he says, "I have to have obedience and respect, and then I can teach." This is backwards. The outside of the cup gets scoured, the inside is ignored. Does the cup just get put on the shelf?

*

Now I would be the first to admit that an obedient child makes a better pupil. But I wonder what I mean by that. Is the child who does what I tell him obedient? What if he only does what I tell him and never what he wants? In that case my electric lawn mower is obedient. In that case obedience means nothing more than predictable mechanical cause and effect.

I can frighten the child into doing what I want him to do. It's easy. I'm bigger. Is he obedient if he's afraid to do other than as I tell him?

These schoolchildren were brought into my classroom and they walked like robots. Four of them. They expected yet again to be programmed. You could have knocked them over with a feather, that's how they appeared. Then I talked to them. Suddenly they were extremely enthusiastic, feverish nearly. Energy, what we sometimes call nervous energy, *happened* to them. This increased in leaps and bounds. After half an hour they could only with great difficulty take in what I said. The so-called energy, more like an anxiety really, had blotted out their sensibility. I could tell that I felt tempted to repress, to shout, to demand order, 'obedience'.

But they were doing nothing wrong. They jumped about after a while, pushed and shoved one another a bit. Now and again they took me up on my suggestion for five or ten minutes, then they were not a group any more but individual youngsters, a little tipsy with freedom; behaving the way tipsy people do. Falling over, ordering each other around, quarrelling, one eye on me sometimes as if wondering: When will the thread snap, when will the trap shut.

I made as sure as I could that no one was hurt. Then I dismissed them. I don' know how they arrived in their regular classroom. But next time I saw them I talked it over with them. This uncontrollable energy, how does it happen? Did they know they were helpless?

*

Our will – our appetite for freedom.

As a parent I have the right to demand obedience from my children. In an emergency I have the duty to demand it. It's a natural right and a natural duty; it isn't legal or social.

I manage to be both parent and teacher to my own children. "You must spend two hours with me between four and six tomorrow afternoon. We are going to do music." So my son arrives at four o'clock sharp, maybe five minutes late, but then he apologizes. That's fine. He obeyed. He was glad to obey because often he enjoys music. But he also obeyed because if he had not obeyed I would have scolded him. He would have found that unpleasant. It would have seemed to interfere with the tie of affection. Every member of our family knows, luckily, at what prize affection is bought and maintained nowadays. There's a great deal of uncanny fear about. None of us know exactly what is going to rise in ourselves next, in terms of temperament, or mood, or malice.

As soon as we 'do music' I put the parent away and bring out the teacher. But I remember that it was the parent who told him to be here so that he could be taught.

*

In terms of our will and of what we want, and with respect to human growth, I prefer to think of education as the ongoing satisfaction of our appetite for freedom. If we study this appetite of the human natural being, how it can be spoiled, how it can rage, turn into a lust, become addictive, disappear altogether as such, we will in fact be concerning ourselves with the why and wherefore of education.

We are quite right to have made a big thing out of it, I think. The son of man must be raised, it comes down to that, which is fundamental humanity in the building.

So shouldn't we be looking at education right from the start as a life-long concern?

If we link education to our appetite for freedom we will get furthest, in my opinion. We should ask: When is this appetite strongest, when does it first show up – and then we should take a close look at the state of it nowadays. I don't think it's right to ignore *how things might be intead*. We may still be suffering a hang-over from those heady days of a spurious idealism, but idealism is not vision. Vision informs us, among other things, of how we can be healthy, sound, happy and perfect. Sometimes those who reject vision and its information do so because they cannot stand the strain of the discrepancy between what might be and what, for them, actually is the case.

*

A child without peace, who has no notion of peace, not even an appetite for it but the first vital impulse disconcerts him, confounds him, makes him reach for his mask – here is where *experimentation* can be useful.

A mature adult, when his soul is worn threadbare, will groan in his agony: God, give me peace! and he will get it, because he knows how to ask and because he believes that when he asks he gets. A confused adult forgets to ask; an immature adult doesn't know how, being too proud, too silly, whatever. Children in that respect are not different. Like adults, they have acquired their defence mechanisms and they may be aware of them or not. Often they have their own way of getting peace, ways we adults have left behind, or we were never aware of them – or we had them trained out of us.

The appetite for freedom, for the peace that makes liberty digestible, exists equally in adults as in children. At any age it can be nourished, informed, spoiled, distorted, created or eradicated.

Children and adults have all the reason in the world to look at each other and say: Yes, I know what you mean, I have the same hang-ups, I suffer from the same setbacks. We both prefer pleasure to pain, don't we, and bliss to injury.

Imagine a conversation such as the following between an adult and a child;

Child: You get angry quick, don't you? I bet that worries you.

Adult: It does indeed. Anger comes over me before I know. I suffer for it afterwards. I wish I had some of your devil-may-care attitude.

Child: Oh, don't think too highly of it. That's my protective gear. I may not lose my temper so often but I feel out of touch. I don't seem to be able to get close up enough to things to really appreciate them. It's frustrating. You know, when I play outside for instance, I start feeling great because I'm in the fresh air and the sunshine and I'm full of ideas about what to do, and then one little thing goes wrong, like Stuart can't come out to join me, and suddenly I just don't care any more. I reach out for that excitement but it disappears.

Adult: That's heart-breaking, isn't it. I know all too well what you mean. I broke off a relationship with my favourite person only a week ago because all we did was argue and fight. Both of us remembered what it used to be like, when we cared for each other. But we couldn't help ourselves. I wish I knew what went wrong!

Child: Or how you could have made it right.

Adult: I guess that's even more important.

Child: Really it's not that you argued and fought and in the light of that you broke off your relationship, but that your relationship gradually broke down, what with all the fighting, and then finally you were forced to admit to each other that it was broken.

Adult: Are you not maybe far too smart for a ten-year-old?

Child: I just know what you mean because we spend time talking to each other. We're friends, aren't we? I learn from you, you learn from me. I have toys, and when they break I fix them, but eventually they wear out. Relationships are like that if we toy with them.

Adult: What should we do with them?

Child: Let them develop because they want to grow. We adapt to them, if we're smart. But it takes so much time!

Adult: But then what's the hurry, eh?

Child: Exactly, what's the hurry.

*

Experimentation begins with the supposition that in spite of appearances to the contrary, communication is possible between adults and children. The sole presupposition is human nature as a common denominator.

The teacher then takes the child in his confidence. The child's manner says: My strength is your strength, my experience is your experience. I put them at your disposal. Leave me no room except what I need to muster my forces.

The child we mean has no appetite for freedom. He has lost his appetite; let's adopt the extreme example. However let's also keep in mind that the child who has lost his appetite for freedom is a slave to his senses. He does not see, but his eyes are drawn to this or to that. He does not hear but his attention is drawn by what makes the most noise.

So how does the teacher invade the sensual being of the child?

That is one thing we mean when we speak about experimentation in the case of education. The teacher is going to invade the sensual being of the child. He is going to break the hold on the will of the child. He is able to do that, and he does it, as soon as the child experiences his, the teacher's, strength as greater than that of his own sensuality. Not that there is any real strength in sensuality, but the point is that the child thinks so and feels so. It has as many reasons and makes up as many justifications for thinking and feeling so as any adult does under similar circumstances, but of course the child has his or her own way of non-reasoning that is probably closed to the adult. That is why there is no possibility of progress on the basis of rational thought or conventional feeling. The teacher's good sense must override the child's bad sense. The teacher's compassion overrides the child's resentment. The teacher's understanding overrides the child's prejudice.

But first the teacher must take the child into his confidence, and he does this most successfully by recognizing the child as a fellow human being.

Is he dealing with a problem child here? You bet he is. There is no greater problem known to man than the extinction of his will and the loss of his appetite for freedom.

I don't describe the particular appearance of this problem child. If I were to do that I would mention that which the teacher intentionally ignores. Take the child with the speech defect, and let's assume that we agree on what a speech defect is. As soon as the adult puts his finger on that defect, even drawing it to the attention of the child, that child's sensuality is strengthened to the degree of that attention. So that's no way to alleviate the problem. – Notice this construction: If the child wants to say something badly enough he will overcome his speech defect.

Why do we say 'badly' enough? The child doesn't experience his sensuality as something bad but as something good. To him it's not a weakness, this defect, but the underlying sensuality of it – that which gives rise to it and expresses itself symptomatically as such – is experienced by him as a strength. That's bad. The teacher knows it's bad. He also knows that he can't make the child see that, especially not that it's bad. But if the child wants to speak badly enough he will speak. He will rely on the strength of the teacher.

*

The exuberance of which the child is capable suddenly is likely to come as a surprise to the teacher, not because he may not have expected it but because he has no way of knowing when. The more experienced teacher will remain expectant for longer.

The essence of the exercise is the liberation of the child's faculties. These faculties, which all stem from the will like branches from the trunk of a tree, cannot function while the will itself is enslaved. If the speech function is impaired we can take for granted that the will is inhibited, and that the inhibition is a moment of sensuality. The exuberance afterwards is sensuousness.

Meanwhile the teacher, whose will is intact, and whose special gift is knowledge, is bound to experience the pupil's moment of sensuality. It may occur to him in a variety of ways. Basically he will see it as something he wants to remove. He cares for the child, so he hates whatever harms the child. Nevertheless he will have to overcome this hate in himself, because it too would lend 'strength' to the impediment. Only love can overcome hate. Love is the most powerful and most subtle of all the faculties that branch from our will, and the teacher knows this. He realizes the crucial importance of his function as a loving human being. In no better way can human being be expressed. In no more efficient way can knowledge be imparted.

So the impediment in the child is overwhelmed by the freedom of the teacher and the sensuality dissolves in the knowledge due to the teacher's love.

*

A quick look at 'sensuality':

If something makes sense it has organic veracity. Whatever makes sense is an addition to our knowledge, and to our body of knowledge.

There is sense experience and there is sensuous experience. Sensual experience, however, is impossible because experience is impossible without growth, while sensuality is the futile attempt to remain with some particular sensation.

Why that should occur to us, to remain with some particular sensation, would be a puzzle if we knew less about our need for pleasure. Growing, both physically in wellbeing and spiritually in bliss, is a pleasure. But why should we ever want that pleasure without growing? Why, instead of growing with pleasure, should we want mere pleasure? Or, on the contrary, why should we ever pander to someone's desire for pleasure without first holding out to him the freedom to grow?

Why evil?

The question makes about as much sense, to me, as: Why should anyone, if he chops wood, ever chop off his finger?

The answer is: It just happens, if you're not careful. The same goes for sensuality. It happens if we're not careful.

Sensuality, and all evil for that matter, becomes a puzzle only for those who think for some reason that growth is a mechanical, automatic thing. It isn't. Growth, in cooperation with it as a human-natural necessity, is also creative skill and talent, and the more we cooperate, the more pleasure we gain. Not that pleasure is the reward. To assume that it is constitutes another aberration. The reward is life, and more life. Pleasure however keeps us ticking over smoothly. It's the oil in the works.

Sensuality is a taste for oil at the expense of life.

The teacher concentrates on growth, on organic progress, and he realizes the importance of knowledge; consequently he sees in sensuality his worst enemy. Not that sensuality only undermines growth. It can equally be seen as an attempt to ignore growth – such as when growth has become more and more difficult due to adverse, externally imposed, circumstances.

A being gives up!

*

How many of the children caught up in our school system have given up on growth? I don't blame the child, I don't blame the school system, but the fact of the matter is that a child is caught up in the system and nothing makes sense. It succeeds neither in the system nor in itself. There is no sense of progress, of getting on from a less to a more interesting terrain, from a lesser to a greater degree of self-possession.

Whoever gives up on growth consoles himself with sensuality. Adults and children are alike in this. The forms of sensuality are legion. Knowing what we know about them, does it make sense to tell anyone not to be sensual, because sensuality is bad, and then punishing him for it? Or would it make more sense to teach that person how to grow?

It makes more sense to show a youngster how to cross the street safely than to punish him for having fallen under a lorry.

Some forms of sensuality are just plain mistakes. Once again we lose track of that little something that is necessary and bang, we end up in some mess. We court disease. We practice asceticism. We criticize, we indulge our morbid curiosity, we neglect a friend or an enemy. We know fine well we're not in the business of cataloguing sins or merits, so all that matters is that we get back on track.

The educator knows how to lead his charges away from their mistakes and out of their dead ends and only rarely does he have to mention the failures.

Then there are the more serious forms of sensuality when someone has given up on growth. All *addictions* are like this. We can't deal with these failures ourselves but we require help from someone. That someone has to be aware of what growth in reality is all about. If he doesn't know that he is going to tinker with our failures, or worse, he is going to disturb our being itself in terms of those failures. What we need, in other words, is a teacher or an educator.

*

Now we return to **experimental education**.

What exactly is experimental about it?

It depends now whether you want to involve your imagination or not. Without it your experiment is no more than a case of try this or try that. You drop something, to see how fast it falls, to see whether it falls or not. Then you arrive at some law which you say you have discovered.

But involve your imagination and it doesn't for a moment allow you to sit back and observe passively. It insists that you participate, that you become the thing you would learn from.

So that's the experiment, then, in reality: that you step out of yourself, and that you demonstrate that you are not too cowardly to do so.

So the teacher, the educator, becomes the pupil.

We have all the capacity to enter into one another's being but we don't very often act from that capacity because we've tried it once or twice minus our imagination and the effects were disastrous. So we prefer to stay idle in our safe house, in our privacy. We harbour our own being, unimaginatively. In fact, imagination is more often than not consigned to the trash heap. And why ?

Because it wants to be wooed. I have found this to be the case very much. Imagination is not the sort of faculty that you switch on and off like a light. You can miss it entirely, if you don't know your way about, and end up with magic. Now magic is popular and if you devote yourself to it you too will be popular and then there is no knowing from what roof they'll throw you when they're finished with you.

There's a vast difference between magic and imagination, and the educator has first hand knowledge of the difference. He avoids the former like the plague and he seeks the latter like a great prize, almost like a living, live thing because he knows he cannot force or cause it without committing sacrifice – which is not in the interest of the educator either.

Sacrifice is not popular, like magic, but it is public. All sacrifice is public. We see not through our own eyes but through the eyes of others. Which means that sacrifice is inorganic. I mean it's not organic, in case another meaning might be drawn from that word. When we sacrifice we don't live in reality but we live up to some approximation of reality. We try to live up to such an approximation. We adhere to principles and to standards, and all the time our organic being cries out for water. It cries out to us with a terrible thirst, and every time we slake that thirst, with some approximation of drink, it comes back seemingly twice as lively.

Sacrifice has nothing to do with education. Magic has nothing to do with it either. The one misses the imagination and the other one tramples it underfoot. What a shame. It adds up to a shameful business. When we sacrifice we are afraid to feel ashamed and the very suggestion of shame makes us scuttle for safety behind some justification. But the people who indulge themselves in magic feel the same way about guilt. They cannot abide it, not in themselves and not in others. One would expect them to feel guilty, and so they do of course, being decent at bottom, but they refuse to countenance that guilt. It must be someone else's, they rush to tell you, or it must be something different altogether.

And the one who likes to sacrifice? Shouldn't we expect him to feel ashamed of himself? After all, hasn't he betrayed his imagination? He has, and now it wants none of him. It turns away and will not know him. Shouldn't he feel ashamed of himself now? He does, actually. But he cannot countenance it. If he could, he would be alright and back on track, but he can't. He can't because he won't and he won't because he can't. There he sits, fixed to his sensuality, a grim spectacle.

Imagination is wooed, simply and patiently.

First of all we have to be organically intact. Hence the patience.

Imagination is true. It doesn't spring from the brain and bypass the heart and the sexuality of man. It's not an exercise in electricity. It's more like the sheep that wait for the true shepherd.

The educator realizes, as he makes contact with his pupils, that he may have to do here with a proportion of the products of magic and sacrifice. He is careful not to criticize but he considers it as part of his task to help his charges to face both guilt and shame with equanimity. So he helps them bear the burden of their guilt and shame. That's the only way he can get them to face up to these skeletons in the closet, to these ghosts in the pantry. He says to his charges: Look, I can do it. Now let's do it together. Then you may even do it yourselves.

Because this is a great liberation that has to precede the coming out of oneself, educationally. We cannot come out of ourselves while we are chained by guilt and glued by shame to our own image of ourselves. That image is composed magically and sustained, even augmented, sacrificially. Don't we mistake that image for ourselves? "Create a positive image for yourself!" says the magician. He stands in front of the classroom full of children and preaches the positive image. His voice is smooth as silk. Or the priest says: "Thou shalt sacrifice! Work hard! First work, then pleasure! Do yourselves proud! Do the school proud!" Meanwhile the magician says: "Look, it's easy, just repeat after me ..."

*

So the educator has to woo the imagination in a child. He does it experimentally. He leaves his own being behind and enters the being of the child. He does this by way of compassion and patience, but mostly by way of something called mercy.

The educator is neither popular nor public, but merciful.

I mean to set these three into a comparative light.

Let's coin a phrase: the merciful experiment.

The educator is bound to come up against the popularity and the publicity of the child. As soon as he does so he has the choice to be merciful. The child will confront him in turns with his popular image and with his public image; or with the obverse of these, it amounts to the same. The child will say to him in a variety of ways: this is how people expect me to think, to feel, and to behave. He will either go along with this or react to it, going against it. In neither case has he the option of being an imaginative human being.

The four children who filed into my classroom: that was how they were expected to come in, one after the other, like little trained puppets, and I could see how they all went along with it, with submissive faces, embarrassed. I didn't have time to look closely at all of them, but it seemed to me that while they felt awkward they were willing enough to abide by a set of rules they had adopted. I asked a few unconventional questions and their responses were by rote. They told me what they imagined I wanted to hear and their responses were alike. They knew the drill and since they liked me rather than disliking me they imagined they would please me by putting on this charade of ... but actually they couldn't help it. It happened to them that way. Twenty minutes later the obverse happened to them. They ran about, went a little crazy, but here the various individuals came into the open, and I was glad to see that, though a little apprehensive of the sudden chaos. I didn't have a discipline problem because I was there on that first day to get to know them just a tiny bit, if possible. I didn't want to get to know their misbehaviour patterns so much as their individual being, and how could I do that while they bombarded me with popularity and publicity?

At first they seemed rather alike, like well-trained puppets, but a bit shame-faced, which I took as an encouraging sign. After twenty minutes one of them kicked and poked a couple of others with a pin, especially when they complained. Another shrank into himself and gazed out the window, his hands squeezed tightly between his crossed legs, a little picture of wistful sadness. Another one wanted to obey at any cost, and when I made a suggestion as to what we all might do, he right away did it and encouraged the others to imitate him. This alarmed me slightly, but I took it on board. The fourth one was willing to fight but he suffered, he was divided in himself, and he flew into a bit of a rage when he was kicked again.

*

The merciful experiment implies a merciful attitude towards the child who misbehaves in terms of what I have called popularity and publicity, rather than a punitive, sacrificial, corrective attitude.

I say that this attitude is implied because I suspect that there is more to the experiment than a permissive negligence in the face of pain and disorder.

I imagined I would say that once the chaos has been parried some creative cause can now come into its own, undisturbed.

But that's all misleading because it doesn't take account of the nature of mercy. Mercy is not permissive negligence, nor is it forgiveness. Mercy is itself a creative operation. When we say creative we always mean the human skill of turning raw material into real matter.

The merciful educator views the publicity and the popularity of the children as raw material. He does not counter sacrifice with sacrifice and magic with magic. The displacement of a lesser by a greater sacrifice, of a weaker by a more powerful magic, is sometimes taken for an advance in education, probably because a change is considered as good as a rest.

So I come to the conclusion that the merciful experiment is an application and a practice, by the educator, of experimental mercy.

How is it experimental?

In that the educator goes out of his way to bring it into practice. He decides that the individual ways of the children should take precedence over his own during the hour of education.

Here is where the educator begins to learn. Because mercy must be learned. It is not earned but learned.

Why do we punish? Because we ourselves are afraid of being punished. Why do we coerce discipline in our charges? Because we ourselves are afraid of being coerced.

*

Mercy is learned at the expense of our self-conceit. While we have a head full of notions as to how we can influence a person to his advantage we are not capable of mercy. Mercy springs not only from the head but also from the informed heart.

And another thing, mercy springs from the heart in relation. That means that we actually have to care for someone else. The merciful educator actually cares for his pupil and has his welfare at heart. I mean his welfare as a person, not as a pupil; as an individual person, not as a cog in the machinery of the system.

That's all much more easily said than done. There comes the inevitable disappointment because of failure, the heartbreak because our best efforts seem to be rejected. But one might as well make one's peace with this unless one wants to follow the wide-open path of mechanical data transfer.

What is called for surely is our active heart, and our disappointment is, and our frustrations are, certain signs that we have a heart and they tell us where it is and even how we might best make use of it.

Mercy is learned while our heart is earned.

Our heart, our emotion and feeling, and the way we get hurt inwardly and then either feel sorry for ourselves, or retaliate, or both – our inability to be yielding without being sloppy at the same time, firm in our intentions without hardening of our heart –

* * *

www.ingramcontent.com/pod-product-compliance
Lightning Source LLC
Chambersburg PA
CBHW070316290526
45791CB00003B/1125